Quick & Short
BOOK REPORTS

developed by Randy Marie Thorne

RANDY MARIE THORNE received a Bachelor of Arts degree in Elementary Education and Drama from New Mexico Highlands University. She is an experienced elementary teacher and has taught several in-service classes in New Mexico. Randy teaches fourth and fifth grades at Taos Pueblo.

Copyright 1990 by THE MONKEY SISTERS, INC.
22971 Via Cruz
Laguna Niguel, CA 92677

ISBN 0-933606-86-9

Quick & Short
BOOK REPORTS

This collection of easy and creative book report forms will be especially helpful to students who find writing book reports a difficult task. Many of the reporting forms will be ideal for younger students' beginning book reporting experiences.

The clever formats and bold graphics combine to make these book reports a fun activity while encouraging students to complete the "Quick & Short" book reports successfully.

TABLE OF CONTENTS

Free Choice Books with a Page Theme

Generic "Free Choice" Book Reports

ANIMAL BOOKS

Title _____

_____

Author _____

_____

Fiction   Circle One   Nonfiction

What kind of animal or animals is this book about?

_____

_____

Write five sentences about this book.

_____

_____

_____

_____

_____

_____

_____

_____

Name _____

BABYSITTING BOOKS

Title _____

Author _____

Characters _____

_____

Tell about a situation in the book that reminded you of an experience you've had babysitting or dealing with younger brothers and sisters.

_____

_____

_____

_____

Describe another problem that occurred.

_____

_____

_____

_____

How was it solved?

_____

_____

_____

_____

Name _____

BIOGRAPHY

What character traits did this person have that helped him or her achieve these accomplishments? List five, and give an example of a time this trait was shown in the book.

_____

_____

_____

_____

_____

_____

_____

_____

_____

_____

_____

_____

Name _____

BIOGRAPHY

Title _____

Author _____

Main Character _____

Setting _____

Why is this person famous?

_____

_____

_____

_____

_____

_____

Name_____

CHARACTER PROFILE

Title _____

Author _____

Character _____

Age_____ Male or Female (circle one)

Describe the character in the book. Tell what you think the character looked like.

_____

_____

_____

_____

What kind of personality did this character have?

_____

_____

_____

_____

What did the character do that you admire?

_____

_____

_____

_____

THE CASE IS SOLVED

Choose one of the cases that you solved and describe it. What steps did you and the detective use to solve the case? What was the solution to the problem?

Crime Report of _____

from the book _____ Page _____

by _____

Name of Case _____

Case description: _____

_____

_____

_____

Steps to solving the case: _____

_____

_____

_____

Solution of case: _____

_____

_____

_____

Name _____

FANTASY

Title _____

Author _____

Was the setting of the book realistic or a fantasy?

Explain why _____

_____

_____

_____

If one of the fantasy happenings in the book could happen in _your_ life, what would it be? How would it change your life?

_____

_____

_____

_____

_____

_____

_____

Name _____

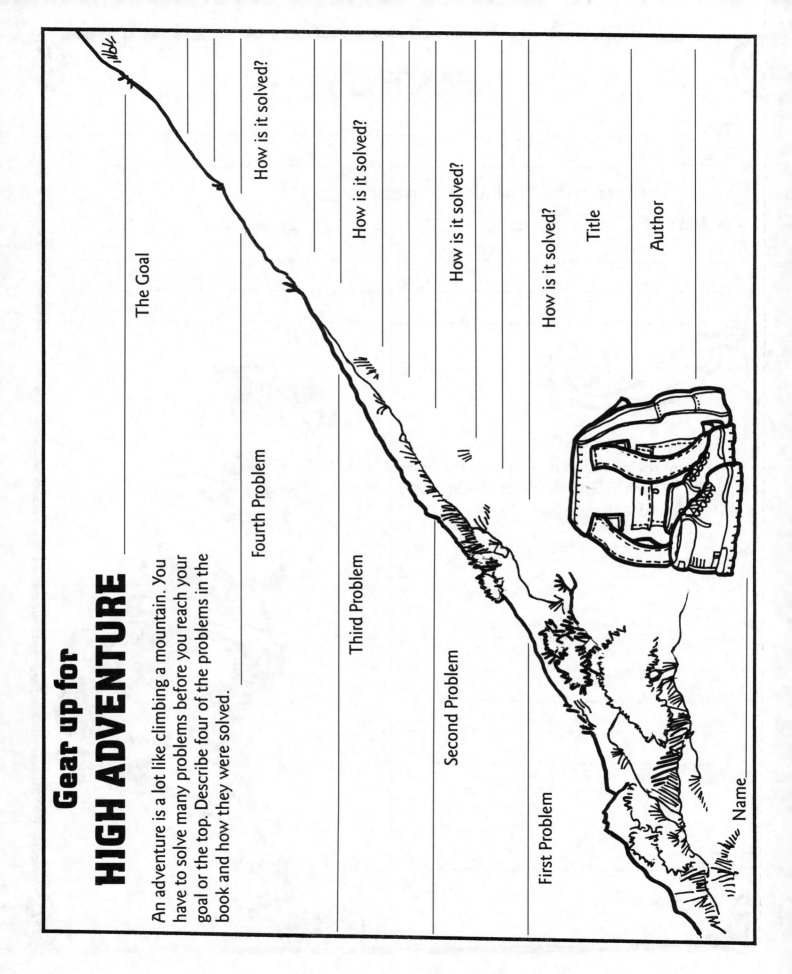

Gear up for
HIGH ADVENTURE

An adventure is a lot like climbing a mountain. You have to solve many problems before you reach your goal or the top. Describe four of the problems in the book and how they were solved.

The Goal

How is it solved?

Fourth Problem

How is it solved?

Third Problem

How is it solved?

Second Problem

How is it solved?

First Problem

Title

Author

Name

HISTORICAL FICTION

Title _____

Author _____

Setting _____

Historical Event _____

How did the historical events affect the main character?

_____

_____

_____

_____

_____

_____

_____

_____

_____

_____

_____

_____

_____

_____

_____

Name _____

JOKE BOOKS

Title ____________________

Author ____________________

What was your favorite joke in this book? ____________________

What makes it funny? ____________________

Write your own joke using the same theme. ____________________

JOKE BOOKS

Name ____________________

Quick and Short Book Reports © THE MONKEY SISTERS, INC.

IT MUST BE MAGIC!

Title _____

Author _____

Perform a magic trick from the book for a friend or family member.
Then answer these questions.

What really happened?

_____

_____

_____

_____

_____

How did they feel when they had been tricked?

_____

_____

_____

_____

_____

Name _____

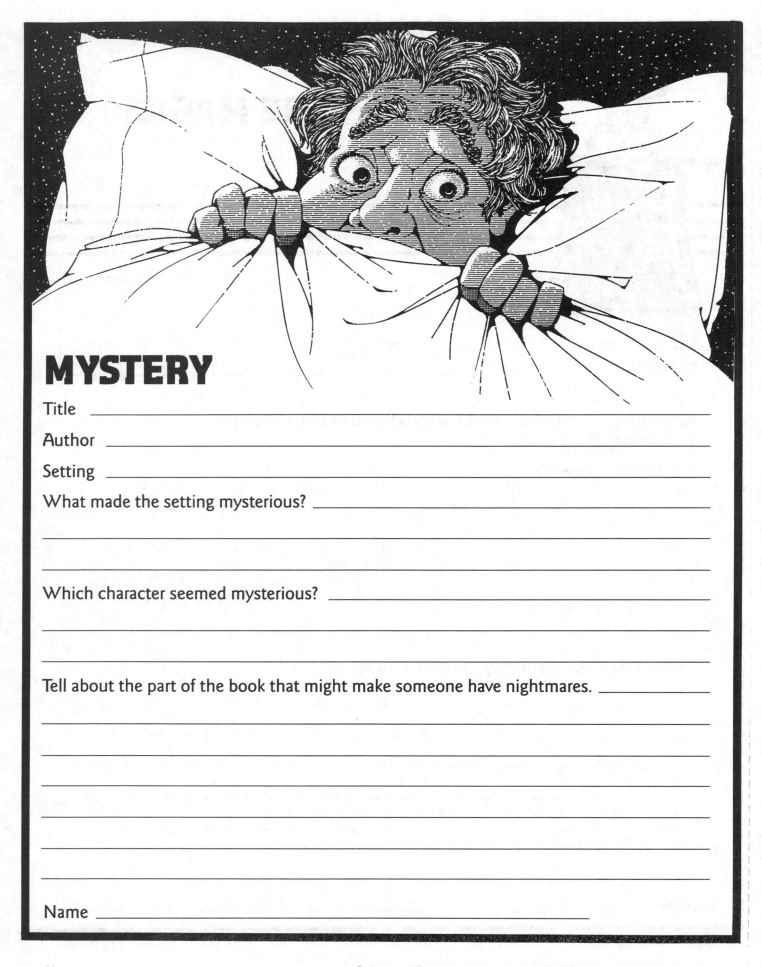

MYSTERY

Title _____

Author _____

Setting _____

What made the setting mysterious? _____
_____
_____

Which character seemed mysterious? _____
_____
_____

Tell about the part of the book that might make someone have nightmares. _____
_____
_____
_____
_____
_____
_____
_____

Name _____

Quick and Short Book Reports © THE MONKEY SISTERS, INC.

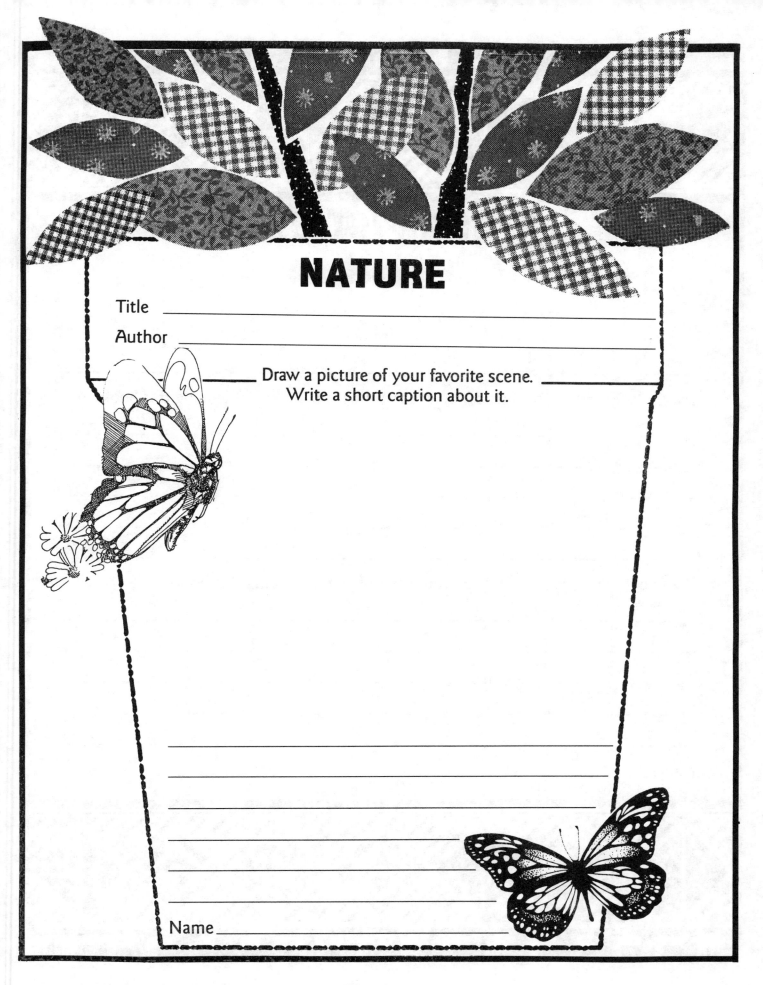

NATURE

Title _____

Author _____

Draw a picture of your favorite scene.
Write a short caption about it.

_____
_____
_____
_____
_____
_____

Name _____

NON-FICTION

Title

_____

Author

_____

List five things that you already knew about this subject before reading this book.

_____

_____

_____

_____

_____

List five things that you learned about this subject by reading this book.

_____

_____

_____

_____

_____

Name_____

A PICTURE BOOK

Draw four pictures of the action in the story and write captions for them.

Title

Author

REALISTIC FICTION

TITLE

_____

AUTHOR

_____

SETTING

_____

CHARACTERS

_____   _____

_____   _____

_____   _____

What parts of this book seemed real? _____

_____

_____

_____

_____

_____

What parts of this book seemed fake or unreal? _____

_____

_____

_____

_____

_____

Name _____

SCIENCE EXPERIMENTS

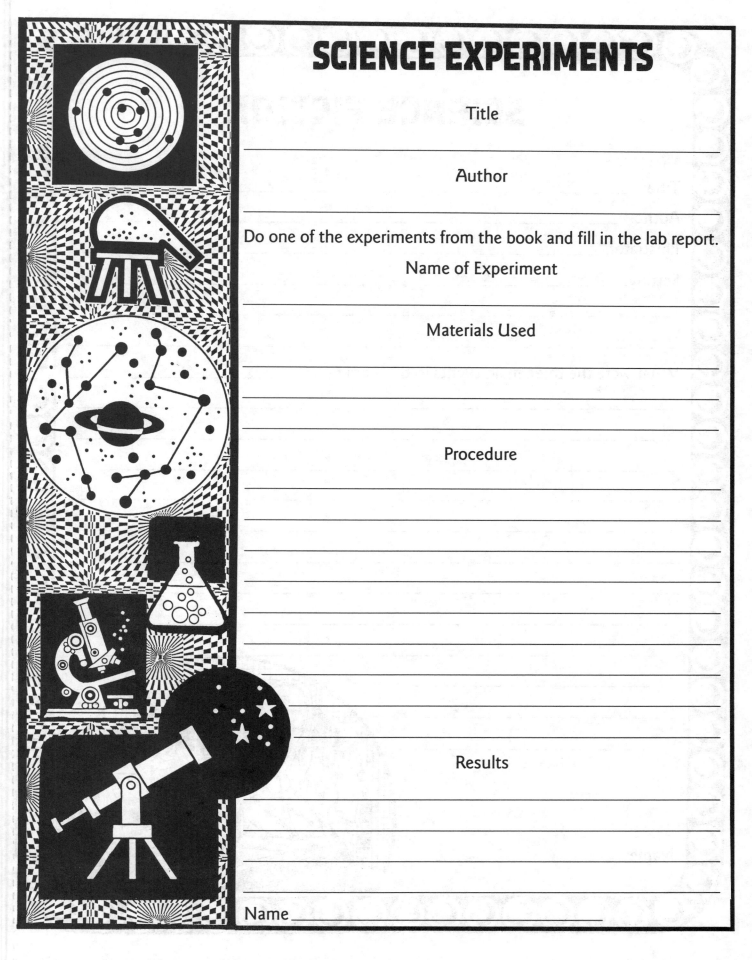

Title
_____

Author
_____

Do one of the experiments from the book and fill in the lab report.

Name of Experiment
_____

Materials Used
_____
_____
_____

Procedure
_____
_____
_____
_____
_____
_____
_____
_____
_____

Results
_____
_____
_____

Name _____

SCIENCE FICTION

Title: _____

Author: _____

Illustrator: _____

Setting: _____

_____

_____

What were the three main events in this book? _____

_____

_____

_____

_____

_____

_____

_____

_____

_____

_____

Name _____

SHORT STORIES

Title _____

Author _____

Choose two of your favorite stories to compare and contrast. List 5 ways that the stories are alike and different.

Title of story_____

Title of story_____

Alike

_____
_____
_____
_____
_____
_____
_____
_____
_____
_____
_____
_____
_____

Different

_____
_____
_____
_____
_____
_____
_____
_____
_____
_____
_____
_____
_____

Name_____

THINK BIG!

TALL TALES

Title _____

Author _____

Characters _____

In many stories the main character is bigger than life and performs extraordinary feats. List three ways that the main character is bigger than life and the feats he does because of them.

_____

_____

_____

_____

_____

_____

_____

_____

_____

Name _____

SOLVE A PROBLEM
ON THE
BOOK REPORT MACHINE

BOOK REPORT MACHINE

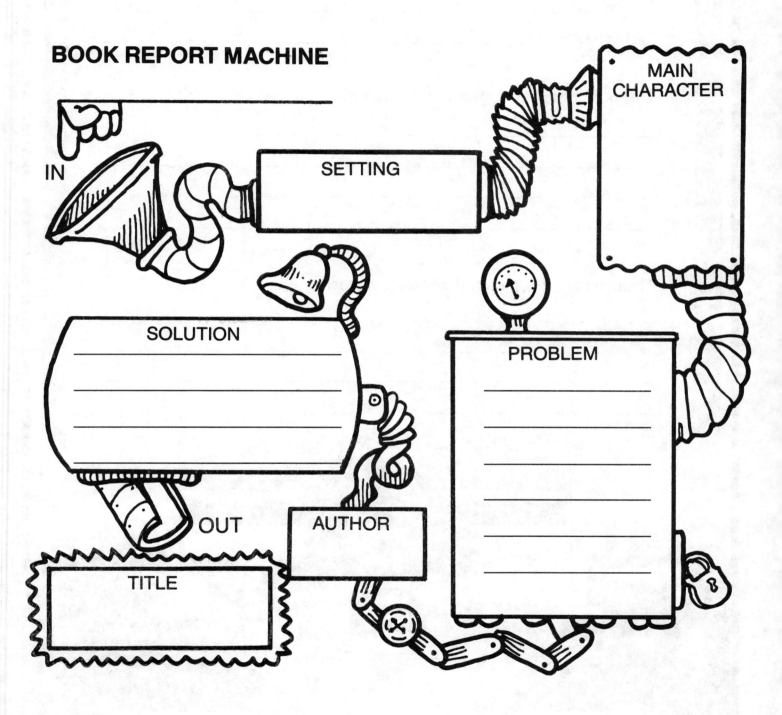

IN

SETTING

MAIN CHARACTER

SOLUTION

PROBLEM

OUT

AUTHOR

TITLE

Name _____

RACING READER

Title _____

Author _____

Racing Reader _____

This book deserves to be a winner because _____

_____

_____

_____

_____

The most exciting part of the book was when _____

_____

_____

_____

_____

Name _____

Fill in the timeline with events that happened in the story.

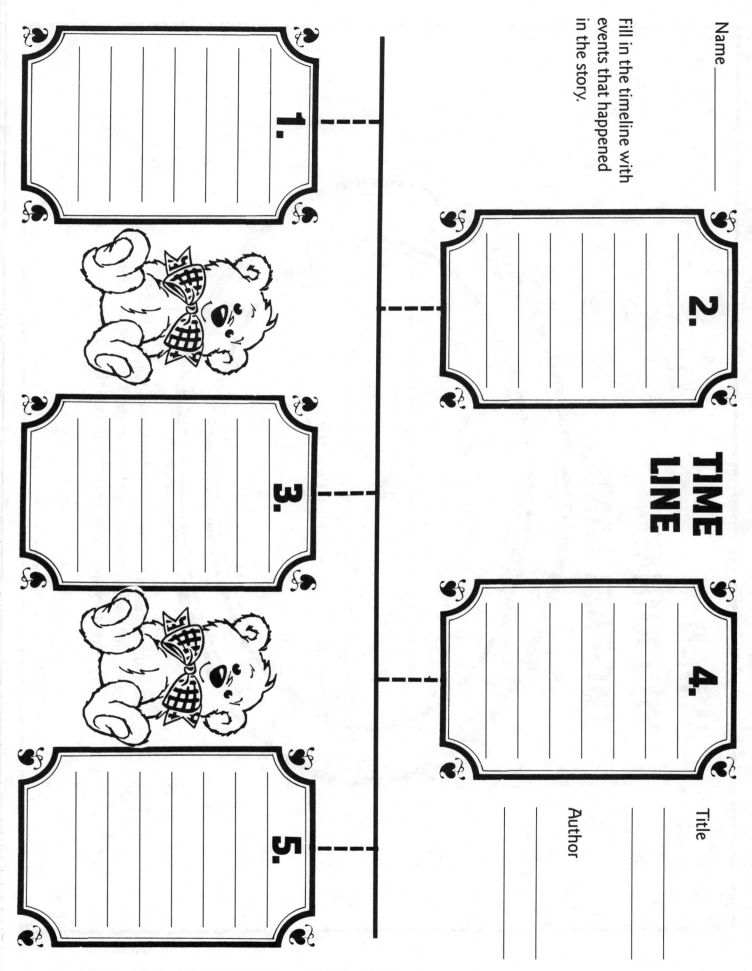

TIME LINE

1.

2.

3.

4.

5.

Title _____

Author _____

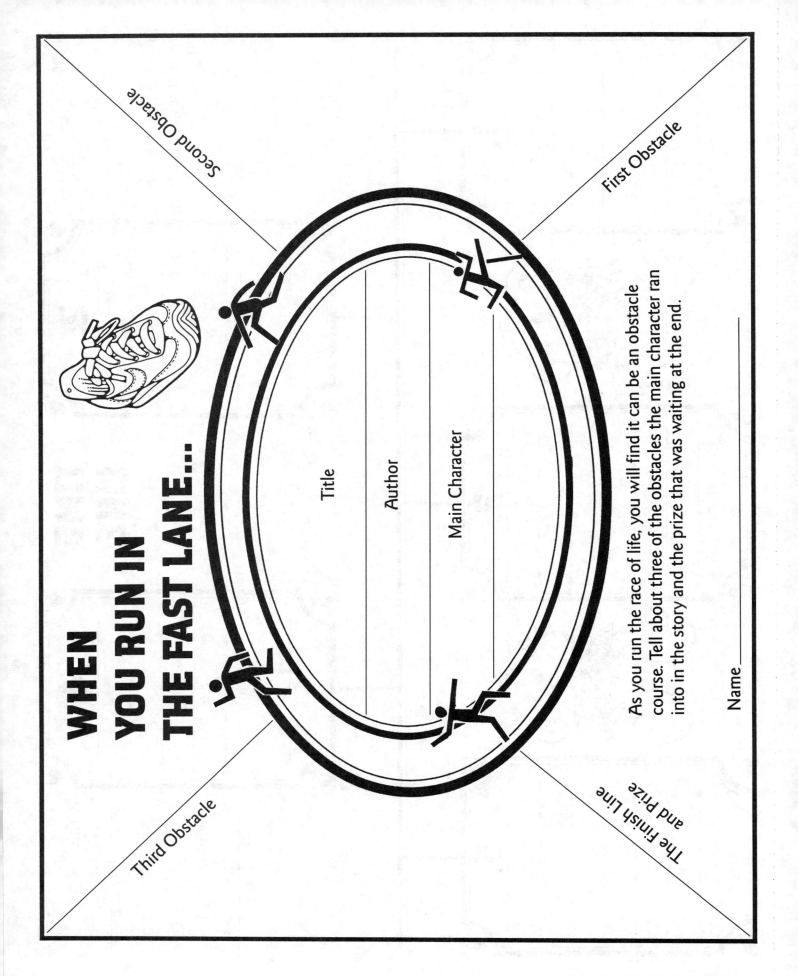

WHEN
YOU RUN IN
THE FAST LANE...

First Obstacle

Second Obstacle

Third Obstacle

The Finish Line
and Prize

Title

Author

Main Character

As you run the race of life, you will find it can be an obstacle course. Tell about three of the obstacles the main character ran into in the story and the prize that was waiting at the end.

Name _____

A LITTLE

EXTRA EFFORT

MAKES THE DIFFERENCE

Title _____

Author _____

Main Character _____

Tell about a time when the main character made a
little extra effort that made a difference.

_____

_____

_____

_____

_____

_____

_____

_____

What would have happened if that extra effort would
not have been made?

_____

_____

_____

_____

_____

_____

_____

_____

Name _____

POST CARD BOOK REPORTS

When you read a book, you are taken on a little "mind trip" or vacation into someone else's world or life. Write a post card to a friend describing the places you've visited and the people you've met while reading this book. Make your friend wish they were there with you!

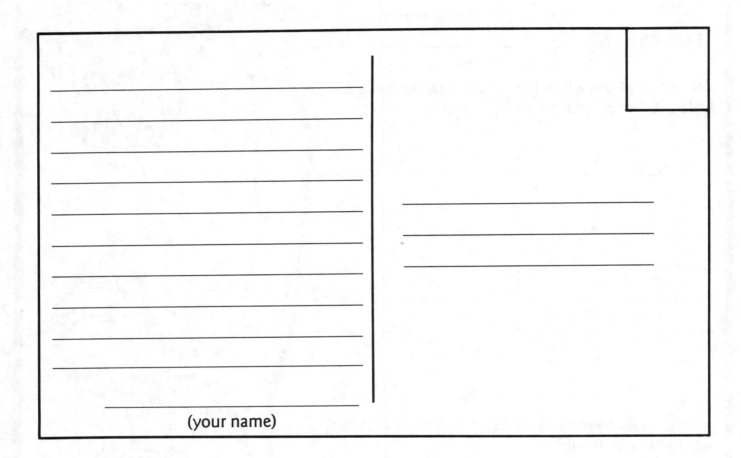

(your name)

Illustrate your post card on the other side to show an inviting scene from the book. Include the title and author in the artwork.

DROP 'EM A LINE

Title _____

Author _____

Write a letter from the main character to a good friend describing some of the most interesting events that happened to him or her.

_____

_____

_____

_____

_____

_____

_____

_____

_____

_____

_____

_____

_____

Name _____

WRITE-A-POEM!

Title _____

Author _____

Write a poem about the book. Use whatever form of poetry works for you—
haiku, tanka, sonnet, ladder poems, rhymed poems, rap, diamonte, etc.

_____

_____

_____

_____

_____

_____

_____

_____

_____

_____

_____

_____

_____

_____

_____

_____

Name _____

REPORT CARD
BOOK REPORT

Pretend you are the main character's teacher. What kind of report card will you send home after having this character in your classroom? Be sure to write a comment to the parents.

For: _____
(student/character)

Homeroom: _____
(title of book)

Date: _____

Reading	
Language	
Math	
Spelling	
Science	
Social Studies	
Conduct	

Comments: _____

_____

_____

_____

_____

Sign and return: _____
(your name)

LITTLE BOOK BOOK REPORT

Directions:

TO THE TEACHER: This manipulative activity is similar to the Japanese paper-folding art of Origami. It will require teacher-directed assistance. Prior to doing this with your students, it is suggested that you duplicate 3-4 copies of the following page and practice the cutting and folding to make a correct completed sample to use with your students. Once you have made a correct sample, it is suggested that you work with small groups of students around a table so they can see how to follow the directions close up.

1. Cut out on thin-line border.

2. Fan-fold the paper across the shorter (7½-inch) horizontal lines. Open and fold along the longer (9⅞-inch) vertical line so that the pages are facing you as you fold.

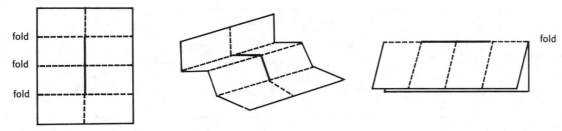

3. Open the paper and fold it in half across the middle 7½-inch dotted line. Cut along the center dark line through both halves. This is a 2½-inch cut.

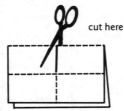

4. Unfold and re-fold in half horizontally across the 9⅞-inch length.

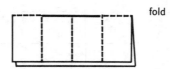

5. Fold the ends in so that page 2 is back-to-back to page 3 and page 6 is back-to-back with the back cover. See the illustration below of the view looking down from the top of a completed little book. (If correctly assembled, the front cover and back cover will be side-by-side facing the back when the book is standing.)

CLOSE THE PAGES TO FORM A BOOK

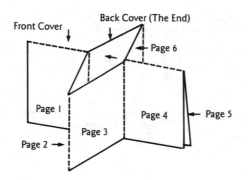

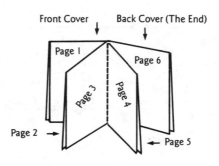

Quick and Short Book Reports © THE MONKEY SISTERS, INC.

LITTLE BOOK
BOOK REPORT

By

1.

Title

Author

2.

The Main Character

3.

The best part of
the book is when . . .

The End

6.

My Favorite Scene

5.

The Setting

4.

OLD WAYS — NEW WAYS

Title

_____

Author

_____

Find five examples in the book of doing things in an old-fashioned way.
Then tell how it is done today.

Old Way	New Way
_____	_____
_____	_____
_____	_____
_____	_____
_____	_____
_____	_____
_____	_____
_____	_____
_____	_____
_____	_____
_____	_____

Name _____

CITY BOOKS

Title

_____

Author

_____

Characters

_____

_____

List 5 phrases from the book describing the city setting of the book.

_____

_____

_____

_____

_____

What incidents or events would not have happened in this book if they would have happened in the country?

_____

_____

_____

_____

Name _____

COUNTRY BOOKS

Title

_____

Author

_____

Characters

_____

_____

List five phrases from the book describing the country setting of the book.

_____

_____

_____

_____

_____

What items or events would not appear in this book if it would have happened in the city?

_____

_____

_____

_____

_____

Name _____

Title _____

Author _____

Write about the most *treemendous* part of the book. Don't *leaf* anything out!

_____

_____

_____

_____

_____

_____

_____

_____

_____

_____

_____

_____

_____

_____

_____

Name _____

A TREEMENDOUS BOOK

FEELINGS

List four actions that the main character has to do in the book. Then write how the main character felt as it was being done.

Title _____

Author _____

Setting _____

Main Character _____

Actions	Feelings

Name _____

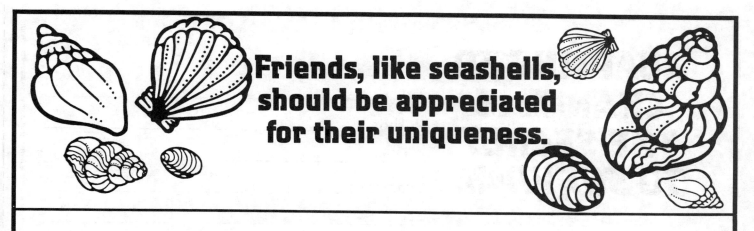

Friends, like seashells, should be appreciated for their uniqueness.

Title _____

Author _____

Characters _____

Tell how your favorite character in this book is unique. Why would it be fun to be friends with this character?

_____

_____

_____

_____

_____

_____

_____

_____

_____

_____

_____

_____

Name _____

ADAPTING TO CHANGE IS THE SECRET TO *SURVIVAL*

Title _____

Author _____

Setting _____

Characters _____

_____

_____

_____

There are many times every day that people need to adapt or adjust to change in their life. Describe one or two situations that show how the main character had to adapt to change.

_____

_____

_____

_____

_____

_____

_____

_____

_____

_____

Name _____

HELP! HELP!

Title _____

Author _____

Characters _____

_____

Setting _____

Describe a time when the main character had a problem and needed help.

_____

_____

_____

_____

_____

What message could have been placed in a bottle asking for help?

_____

_____

_____

_____

_____

Name _____

IMPORTANT MESSAGE
mediately for you

WHAT'S HAPPENING?

Title _____

Author _____

Characters _____

_____

Setting _____

_____

List four events that happened in the book. Then tell what made each event happen in the next column.

Happening	**What Made It Happen?**
_____	_____
_____	_____
_____	_____
_____	_____
_____	_____
_____	_____
_____	_____
_____	_____
_____	_____
_____	_____
_____	_____
_____	_____

Name _____

MAIN EVENTS

Title

_____
_____

Author

_____
_____

Write about two of the main events in the story.

Name _____

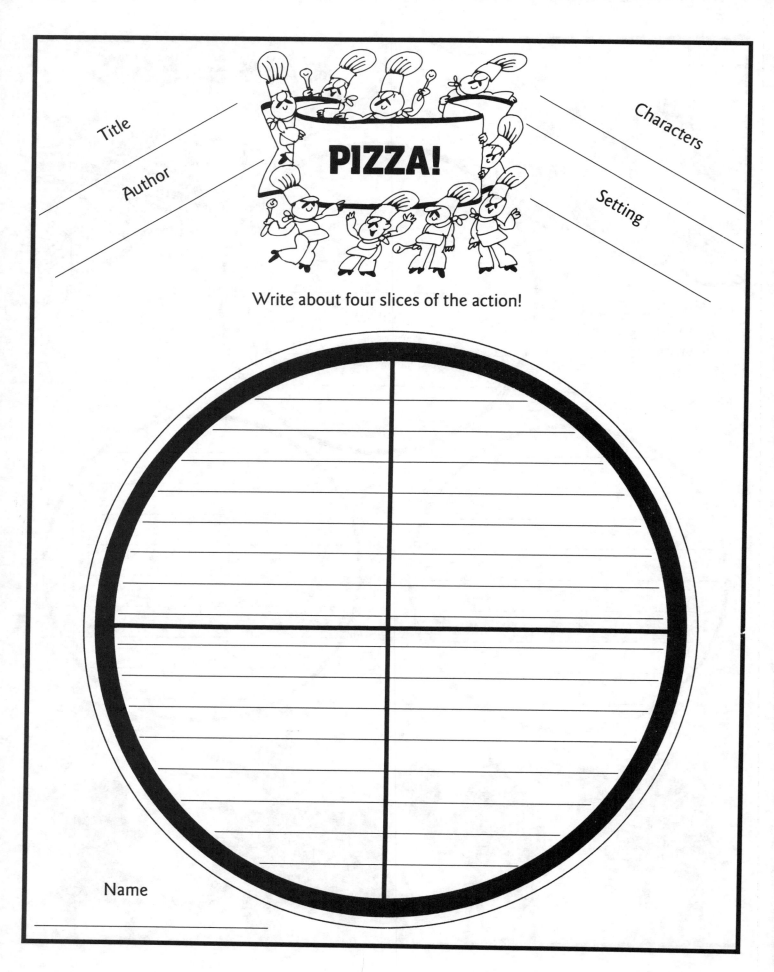

Title

Author

PIZZA!

Characters

Setting

Write about four slices of the action!

Name

HOT DOG!

Title

_____

Author

_____

Setting

_____

Characters

_____

Tell about the best part of the book. Be sure not to leave out the little extras that made you RELISH the book.

_____

_____

_____

_____

_____

_____

_____

_____

It's the little
extras that make
the BIG DIFFERENCE.

Name _____

HERE'S THE LATEST SCOOP!

Title _____

Author _____

Main Character _____

Setting _____

Describe a time when the main character was in a CRUNCH.

_____

_____

_____

_____

What happened to make the situation PEACHES AND CREAM?

_____

_____

_____

_____

Describe a time that was BANANA NUTS.

_____

_____

_____

_____

What flavor of ice cream would you use to describe this book?
Why? _____

_____

_____

_____

Name_____

Quick and Short Book Reports © THE MONKEY SISTERS, INC.

RAINY DAY READING

Title _____

Author _____

When it rains it pours.

Tell about a time in the book when everything seemed to go wrong.

_____

_____

_____

_____

_____

_____

Every cloud has a silver lining.

Tell how everything got straightened out.

_____

_____

_____

_____

_____

_____

Name _____

SING THE STORY!

Title _____

Author _____

Write a song about the book. Use the tune of a well-known song. Be sure to include the main character and your favorite part of the book.
Get together with some classmates and sing the song for your class.
Perhaps your class can have a song contest.

_____
_____
_____
_____
_____
_____
_____
_____
_____
_____
_____

Name _____

MAP A BOOK!

Name _____

Title _____

Author _____

Draw a map of the setting of the book. Be sure to include all of the places where action occurred. Label each place with a symbol and make a map _key_ or _legend_ to show what they stand for.

DESIGN AN AD

Design an advertisement to promote the book. Be sure to include the title and author. The ad should make someone else want to read the book.

Name _____

A BOOK I LOVE!

Author: _____

Title: _____

What did you LOVE about this story?

Name _____

FREE CHOICE

Name _____

Title

_____

Author

_____

Setting

_____

Type of Book

_____

List 20 verbs or action words that show what happened in the story.

_____
_____
_____
_____
_____
_____
_____
_____
_____
_____
_____
_____
_____
_____

Write a sentence describing three main characters. Tell how they looked and acted.

_____
_____
_____
_____
_____
_____
_____
_____
_____
_____
_____
_____
_____
_____

FREE CHOICE

Title _____

_____

Author _____

Write four sentences telling what the story is about.

1. _____

2. _____

3. _____

4. _____

List four main characters and write a sentence telling who each character is.

_____

_____

_____

_____

_____

_____

_____

_____

Name _____

FREE CHOICE

Write four sentences telling what the story is about.

Title

Name

Author

AND THE WINNER IS . . .

Title

Author

Type of Book

Characters

This book is the best book I've ever read!
It is a winner because

Name